# Martyrs' Prayers

*Seeking God in the Midst of Suffering*

Compiled and Translated by

# Duane W.H. Arnold

Reader Hill

Yucaipa, California

*MARTYRS' PRAYERS*
Third Edition
Copyright © 1991, 2002, 2018 by Duane W.H. Arnold
All rights reserved.

(Originally published by Zondervan Publishing House as *Prayers of the Martyrs* in 1991 and then as *Beyond Belief* in 2002)

ALL RIGHTS RESERVED. No part of this text may be reproduced, stored in a retrieval system, scanned, or transmitted, in any form or by any means, electronic, mechanical, photocopying, recording, or otherwise without prior written permission of the publisher. The only exception is the reproduction of brief quotations as part of a review of this work.

Cover Artwork: *The Stoning of St Stephen* by Annibale Carracci, 1603-04

Artworks replicated in this book are all recognized as being in the public domain.

Reader Hill

Published by
Reader Hill
PO Box 490
Yucaipa, CA 92399-0490
www.readerhill.com

Reader Hill logo and colophon are trademarks of Reader Hill.

Dedicated
to
my dear friends,
Dame Angela Ahrendts, DBE
and
Sr. Mary Owen, OSB

I have learned more
from the integrity of
their lives than they
have ever learned
from me.

# Table of Contents

Foreword by Madeline L'Engle ........................ ix
Preface ................................................................ xiii
Praise .................................................................... 1
Preparation ......................................................... 11
Examination ....................................................... 27
Approach ............................................................ 43
Forgiveness ......................................................... 67
Imitation ............................................................. 75
Consummation .................................................. 83
Epilogue ............................................................ 105
Those Who Pray .............................................. 111
Listen to the Songs ......................................... 123

# Foreword

The prayers that Duane Arnold has gathered together are a beautiful compilation of the love of Christian martyrs for their God and the Lord Jesus Christ. This is a book to be sipped, and turned to again and again.

The love of the martyrs is in marked contrast to the fear and hate of those who made martyrs. The words of Shenoufe the Copt in his blessing of Jesus are an affirmation of the love of God that is with us always, in weal and woe. Theodota of Philippopolis gives thanks that she has been counted worthy to suffer in Christ's name, and urges, 'As you showed mercy to Rahab, and received the penitent thief, turn not your mercy from me'.

Who are going to be the martyrs of the last decade of the twentieth century, and who are going to be the persecutors? What has caused people throughout the centuries to want to kill other people for bringing them good news? Surely the news that the first Christian martyrs brought to the world was extraordinarily good: 'God so loved the world that he gave his only begotten Son, that whosoever believeth in him should not perish, but have everlasting life. For God sent not his Son into the world to condemn the world; but that the world through him might be saved.' What could be more wonderful! Yet the news of God's love has always frightened those who believe only in God's wrath.

It is ironic that many of the heresies for which Christians have been burned, stoned, and thrown to wild beasts have been (and still are) heresies of love. It was once a heresy to believe that God in his infinite love surely would not condemn unbaptized infants to the flames of hell - surely a heresy of love. Montanus affirms that 'we all have the same spirit, and this is what unites us in our actions and all that we do together. . . To be your children, we must love one another'. Another heresy of love.

The martyrs of the 1990s may well also affirm heresies of love, and their persecutors may not be people who do not believe in Christ as Lord, but in those who call themselves Christians. There is a sad tendency today for Christians to seek to condemn other Christians and to read books not looking for love and courage, or with any regard for content, but looking for ugliness and for Satan. We do tend to find what we look for. If we look for Satan we will find Satan, and that is dangerous indeed. As Christians, we must look for Christ, and for love. Nemesian of Numidia cries out, 'Let us help each other by our prayers, so that God and Christ and the whole choir of angels may come to our aid in our time of suffering, when we shall need their assistance the most'.

Indeed we need to help each other in this last decade of a troubled century. We know far more about the nature of God universe than we did a century ago, and this knowledge of the wonders of God's glory is frightening to some people who want to hang on to the old human-centered way of looking at what God has made. There is a new and troublesome fear of the imagination -though without it, how can anyone believe in the Incarnation, the Power that created all of the galaxies willingly limiting itself to be one of us for love of us! And this fear is expressing itself in a new kind of book burning and witch-hunting.

Jesus called us to be loving, to be vulnerable, to be as little children, and it is a calling too frightening for those who insist on living with certainty. The martyrs throughout the ages have known terrible uncertainty redeemed by that perfect love that casts out fear. Clement of Rome speaks deeply to my heart when he says, 'Almighty God, Father of our Lord Jesus Christ, grant we pray, that we might be grounded and settled in your truth by the coming of your Holy Spirit into our hearts. What we do not know, reveal to us; what is lacking within us, make complete; that which we do know, confirm in us; and keep us blameless in your service, through Jesus Christ our Lord'.

The loving hearts of many martyrs causes them to pray for those who persecute them, as Jesus taught us that we should. Thelica of Abitine pleads, 'O God most high, do not consider the actions of my persecutors as sin. God, have pity on them'. Perhaps the most heartrending of all such prayers is one found in the clothing of a dead child at Ravensbruck concentration camp, which begins, 'O Lord, remember not only the men and women of good will, but also those of ill will', and ends, 'When our persecutors come to be judged by you, let all of these fruits which we have borne be their forgiveness'.

And Archbishop Oscar Romero writes of his persecutors, 'You may say, if they succeed in killing me, that I pardon and bless those who do it. . . . A bishop will die, but God's Church, which is the people, will never perish'.

And Anglican Bishop Hassan Dehqani-Tefti almost echoes the child at Ravensbruck, 'O God, our son blood has multiplied the fruit of the Spirit in the soil of our souls; so when his murderers stand before thee on the day of judgement remember the fruit of the Spirit by which they have enriched our lives. And forgive'.

> Forgive. Love. Seek for the Truth that will give
> us life and life more abundantly.
> Trust is the message that these
> prayers leave with us, a
> message crucial
> for our
> time.

# Madeleine L'Engle
1989

# Preface

Late in the second century of the Christian era, Tertullian wrote that 'the blood of the martyrs is the seed of the Church'. Certainly, martyrdom was no stranger to those Christians who lived and died beneath the sway of a feckless and inconsistent imperial authority during the first three hundred years of the Church earthly pilgrimage. During those three centuries countless thousands of the faithful made the ultimate sacrifice of life itself in a long series of sporadic local, regional, and even empire-wide persecutions that often seemed to have neither rhyme nor reason as to their initiation or cessation. Secular historians have, on occasion, interpreted the zeal for martyrdom among early Christians as deliberate masochism or self-induced suffering. Such an analysis fails to appreciate the theological integrity of the early Church's understanding of what it meant to be a witness - martyria - literally one who shows forth Christ's passion in life and death.

Furthermore, it is wrong to think of martyrdom only within the context of the early Church. In every new land where Christian missionaries have made their way, martyrs, once again, have planted the fields for an ultimate harvest with their blood. From the first forays into the northern and eastern regions of Europe, to the later missions in Asia, the Americas, Australia, and Africa, martyrs have continued to play their part in the continuing saga of the Church. Moreover, the political chaos that has often characterized the development of the modern nation-state has often compelled Christians of a wide variety of confessions to lay down their lives for the sake of conscience or those particular values of human dignity that pertain to the gospel of Christ. There now seems to be common agreement that these too must be counted among the martyrs of the Church.

The criteria stated above have informed the selection of prayers that are presented in this small book. This collection of prayers, however, should not be considered as exhaustive, but only as suggestive of those innumerable pleas, petitions, and praises that have been poured out to God by those who ultimately offered their very lives for the sake of Christ. In this present selection, many of the prayers come from actual eyewitness accounts of trials and executions; some are from the writings set down by the martyrs themselves before their time of sacrifice; others are taken from traditional martyrologies; and a few have been located in biographical studies. All are unique testaments of faith and assurance. Where it has seemed proper and practical, the prayers have been adapted for contemporary usage. The vast majority of the prayers have been newly translated from their original languages for inclusion in this volume.

The prayers have been divided into the 'stages of martyrdom' with a preface of praise and an epilogue of reflective intercessions. The 'stages' are not consistent in every martyrological narrative, but are evident enough to constitute a loose pattern for the purposes of this volume. Preparation contains the prayers of the martyrs in considering persecution and death in advance of the events themselves. Examination considers the confessions of faith in prayer undertaken by the martyrs before their persecutors. Approach puts forward the prayers of the martyrs as their death becomes ever more certain. Forgiveness reflects the compassion of the martyrs toward those who bear the responsibility for their ill-treatment and death. Imitation indicates the awareness of the martyrs that the ' servant is not above his or her lord' and that their death is connected with that of Christ himself. Consummation constitutes the final act in the drama of martyrdom.

The last twenty years have seen a resurgence in that drama. In Africa, a continent in which the Church is growing at a rapid rate surpassing that of the Americas and Europe, martyrdom has become an ever increasing reality. In Asia, national, ethnic and religious majorities continue the persecution of a rapidly growing Christian minority. In the Middle East, resurgent militant forms of Islam have sought the forced conversion of Christians, the destruction of Christian communities (both ancient and modern) and, have stained the ground with the blood of untold Christian martyrs. The reality of martyrdom remains as do the prayers of those who die for the faith of Christ. Be assured, their prayers will join those which we offer in this small collection and, like those who went before them, their prayers will be heard by a loving and gracious God.

In compiling a collection of this sort, I have received much encouragement from friends and colleagues. I especially wish to thank the Rev'd Dr. William Weinrich who first opened to me the world of the martyrs, and my editors, Rachel Boulding (now of blessed memory), Bob Hudson, and Eric Lorenzen.

>
> These prayers are offered to the reader in the hope that those of us who follow Christ today may take upon ourselves the qualities
> of faith, trust, steadfastness, love, and,
> above all, hope, that so typify the
> martyrs and confessors of
> the Church - past,
> present, and
> future.

July 14, 2018
The Feast of John Keble
Priest

Ð.W̊.Ḩ.Ą.
The Scarlet Maples

*The Crucifixion With Scenes of Martyrdom of the Apostles*
by Frans Francken the Younger (17th Century)

# Praise

The glorious company of apostles praise you.
The noble fellowship of prophets praise you.
The white-robed army of martyrs praise you.

## Te Deum Laudamus

# The Eternal Kingdom

The eternal kingdom is within sight,
   a kingdom that shall suffer no loss.
Lord Jesus Christ, we are Christians,
   we are your servants;
You alone are our hope,
   the hope of all Christians.
God almighty, God most high:
   we give you praise,
   we give praise to your name.

## Thelica of Abitine

# The Honor of Your Name

We offer you our simple praise, Lord Jesus,
   for, unworthy as we are,
You have defended us from the errors of the pagans,
   and in your mercy,
You have allowed us to come to this time of suffering
   for the honor of your name.
As you have permitted us to share in the glory
   of your saints,
We offer you glory and praise
   and we commend to your keeping our lives and our souls.

## Lucian of Antioch

Lucian of Antioch
by Anonymous, from the *Menologion of Basil II* (985)

# I Bless You, Jesus

I bless you, Jesus,
   to you belong all blessings.
I bless you, Jesus,
   you are the only begotten of the Father.
I bless you, Jesus,
   you are the true vine,
   the crown upon the throne of the Father.
I bless you, Jesus,
   you walked upon the water,
   and your feet remained dry.
I bless you, Jesus,
   you made the bitter waters sweet.
I bless you, Jesus,
   you are the staff held by the Father.
I bless you, Jesus,
   you are the unmovable rock.
I bless you, Jesus,
   you command the angels.
I bless you, Jesus,
   and your good Father, in whose hands
   is our breath, and who gives us life.
For yours is the power and the glory, forever.
Amen.

## Shenoufe the Copt

# For This, O Christ, I Thank You

For this, O Christ, I thank you.

Keep me in your care,
    for I am suffering, owing to my faith in you.
I worship the Father, the Son, and the Holy Spirit.
I worship the Holy Trinity,
    apart from you there is no other God.
For this, O Christ, I thank you.

Lord, the glory you receive from those whom you
    in your mercy have summoned, is great.
Lord, protect all of your servants:
    remain with them until the end,
    for then they will glorify your name for all eternity.

For this, Lord Jesus Christ, I give you thanks:
    your strength has sustained me;
You have kept my soul from perishing;
    you have granted to me grace, the grace of your name.
Now complete that which has been begun in me
    and by this put the Adversary to shame.

## Euplus the Deacon

# The Greater Crown

I worship you, O Christ,
 and I thank you that I have been
counted worthy to suffer for your name.

Let me grasp the greater crown.

As you showed mercy to Rahab,
 and received the penitent chief,
turn not your mercy from me.

## Theodota of Philippopolis

# I Will Worship

God, you are with me
    and you can help me;
You were with me when I was taken,
    and you are with me now.
You strengthen me.

The God I serve is everywhere -
    in heaven and earth and the sea,
but he is above them all,
    for all live in him:
All were created by him,
    and by him only do they remain.

I will worship only the true God;
    you will I carry in my heart;
No one on earth shall be able to
    separate me from you.

## Quirinus of Siscia

# My Comfort

Jesus Christ is my comfort.
It is you who created us all.
There is only you, one God,
    Father, Son, and Holy Spirit,
        to whom homage and praise are due.

## Januarius of Cordova

*Saint Januarius Shows His Own Relics*
by Louis Finson (1610-12)

# Christ is Risen!

Christ is risen:
   The world below lies desolate.
Christ is risen:
   The spirits of evil are fallen.
Christ is risen:
   The angels of God are rejoicing.
Christ is risen:
   The tombs of the dead are empty.
Christ is risen indeed from the dead,
   The first of the sleepers.
Glory and power are his forever and ever.
   Amen.

## Hippolytus of Rome

# Preparation

If martyrdom consists in confessing God, then every person who conducts himself with purity in the knowledge of God and who obeys his commandments is a martyr in his life and in his words: for in whatever way his soul is separated from his body, he will pour out his faith like blood, both during his life and at the moment of his death. This is what the Lord says in the Gospel: 'Whoever leaves his father, his mother, his brothers, his wife, or his lands, because of the Gospel and my name', such a man is blessed because he has realized in himself not only an ordinary martyrdom, but the true knowledge of martyrdom, in living and acting according to the rule of the Gospel, out of love for the Lord. For the true knowledge is to know the Name and to understand the Gospel.

## Clement of Alexandria

*Sir Thomas More*
by Hans Holbein, the Younger (1527)

# IN ALL MY FEAR

Good Lord, give me the grace,
   in all my fear and agony,
To have recourse to that great fear
   and wonderful agony that you, my Savior,
Had at the Mount of Olives before your
   most bitter passion;
And in meditating thereon,
   to conceive spiritual comfort
   and consolation profitable for my soul.

THOMAS MORE

# The Sheep of Your Pasture

Lord, we beseech you to help and defend us.
Deliver the oppressed, pity the poor,
   uplift those who have fallen,
   be the portion of those in need,
   return to your care those who have gone astray,
   feed the hungry, strengthen the weak,
   and break the chains of the prisoners.
May all people come to know that you only are God,
   that Jesus Christ is your child,
   and that we are your people and
   the sheep of your pasture.

## Clement of Rome

*The Martyrdom of Saint Clement*
by Fungai (1480)

# That Our Fruit May Abound

May God the Father,
    and the everliving high priest Jesus Christ,
strengthen us in faith, truth, and love;
    and give to us our portion among the saints
    with all those who trust in our Lord Jesus Christ.
We pray for all saints, for kings and governors,
    for the enemies of the cross of Christ and
    for ourselves;
We pray that our fruit may abound and that
    we might be made complete in Christ Jesus our Lord.

## Polycarp of Smyrna

*Saint Polycarp*
by Michael Burghers (1685)

# Help Me to Pray

O God, early in the morning I cry to you.

Help me to pray,
    and to concentrate my thoughts on you:
I cannot do this alone.

In me there is darkness,
But with you there is light;
I am lonely,
    but you do not leave me;
I am feeble in heart,
    but with you there is help;
I am restless,
    but with you there is peace.
In me there is bitterness,
    but with you there is patience;
I do not understand your ways,
    but you know the way for me . . .

Restore me to liberty,
And enable me so to live now
    that I may answer before you and before me.
Lord, whatever this day may bring,
Your name be praised.

Dietrich Bonhoeffer

# The Bond of Love

We all have the same spirit,
   and this is what unites us in our actions
   and all that we do together.
This is the bond of love that puts evil to flight
   and that which is most pleasing to God;
It is by our praying together that we receive
   what we ask.
These are the ties that link our hearts together,
   and make mere mortals the children of God.
To inherit your kingdom, 0 God,
   we must be your children;
To be your children,
   we must love one another.

## Montanus and his Companions

# No Other Object

I have no home but the world,
 no bed but the ground,
no food but what Providence sends me
 from day to day,
and no other object but to do your will
 and suffer,
if need be, for the glory of Jesus Christ
 and for the eternal happiness
of those who believe in his name.

## Francis de Capillas

# All My Earthly Happiness

I know the sorrow I will bring to my family.
It has cost me tears of blood to take such a step
  and give those I love such pain.
Who is there who cared for home
  and family more than I?
All my earthly happiness was to be found there.
But you, O God, who united us with such
  tender affection,
weaned me from what I loved that
  I might serve you.

## Theophanes Venard

*Theophane Venard*
by unknown artist (1860)

# I Am Willing

Lord, I seek little of this
   world's wealth.
If I may only be allowed to live and
   serve you, I would be content.
If, however, this seems too much
   in the eyes of those who persecute me,
I am willing to give up my life
   before I forsake my faith.

### Ferreolus of Vienne

# A Stream Flows

My desires are crucified,
   the warmth of my body is gone.
A stream flows
   whispering inside me;
Deep within me it says:
   Come to the Father.

## IGNATIUS OF ANTIOCH

# A Bidding Prayer

Let us help each other
   by our prayers,
so that God and Christ
   and the whole choir of angels,
may come to our aid
   in our time of suffering,
when we shall need their
   assistance the most.

## Nemesian of Numidia

# If I Live...

Let me be steadfast in my faith
   to the end.
I have no hope of seeing my brethren
   again in this life.
If they kill me, let me die
   as a witness to my faith;
If I live, let me go on
   proclaiming it.


Gabra Michael

# Strengthen my Soul

O God, who was and is,
>   you willed that I should be born.
You brought me to salvation
>   through the waters of baptism.
Be with me now and strengthen my soul
>   that I will not weaken.
Praise to God who has looked upon me
>   and delivered me from my enemies.

## Crispina of Thagara

*Procession of the Holy Virgins and Martyrs*
by the Master of Sant'Apollinare (before 526)

# May their Rage Subside

We pray that the God whom the enemies
   of the church are always provoking
   would tame their unruly hearts.
May their rage subside and peace
   return to their hearts;
May their minds, clouded by sin,
   turn and see the light;
May they seek the prayers of the bishop
   and not his blood.

## Cyprian of Carthage

# That I may Attain

I know what must be done.
Only now am I beginning to be a disciple.
May nothing of powers visible or invisible
    prevent me,
that I may attain unto Jesus Christ.
Come fire and cross and grapplings
    with wild beasts,
the rending of my bones and body,
    come all the torments of the wicked one upon me.
Only let it be mine to attain unto Jesus Christ.

## Ignatius of Antioch

# Examination

All Christian virtues, being protestations of our faith and proofs of our fidelity to God, are a true motive of martyrdom.

Alban Butler

*Rome, a view of the river Tiber looking south with the Castel Sant'Angelo and Saint Peter's Basilica beyond*
by Rudolf Wiegmann (1834)

# Christ is in my Heart

There is but one king that I know;
    It is he that I love and worship.
If I were to be killed a thousand times
    for my loyalty to him,
    I would still be his servant.
Christ is on my lips,
Christ is in my heart;
    no amount of suffering will take him from me.

## Genesius of Rome

# Grounded and Settled

Almighty God, Father of our Lord Jesus Christ,
> grant, we pray, that we might be grounded
> and settled in your truth by the coming of
> your Holy Spirit into our hearts.

What we do not know,
> reveal to us;

What is lacking within us,
> make complete;

That which we do know,
> confirm in us;

And keep us blameless in your service,
> through Jesus Christ our Lord.

## Clement of Rome

# The Crown of the Martyr

Lord, grant me this crown for which I have longed;
   for I have loved you with all my heart and all my soul.
I long to see you, to be filled with joy, and to find rest.
Then I will no longer have to witness the suffering of my
   congregation, the destruction of your churches,
   the overthrow of your altars, the persecution of your priests,
   the abuse of the defenseless, the departure from truth,
   and the large flock I watched over diminished by this
   time of trial.
I no longer wish to see those I considered my friends change
   within their hearts, becoming angry and seeking my death;
   or have those who are my true friends taken from me by
   this persecution, while their killers order us about.

Even so, I intend to endure and show my vocation openly in the
   course that is set before me, so that I may be an example
   to all.
I have had the place of honor at the table;
   I shall also have the place of precedence when it comes to
   dying - I will be the first to offer my blood.
I will then enter with my brothers into that life which knows
   no troubles, no cares, no worries;
   a life in which there will be neither persecutors
   nor persecuted, neither oppressor nor oppressed,
   neither tyrants nor victims.
In that life I will find neither the threats of kings nor
   the insults of prefects;

(cont. next page)

no tribunal will judge me or cause me to fear,
no violence or coercion will be found.

Once I have set my steps in your way, I will stumble no more.
There, my weary body will find healing and rest, for the
    Anointed One will be the oil placed upon us.
My heart's anguish will fade when I partake of you,
    the Chalice of our salvation.
My Joy and my Consolation, you will wipe away the tears
    from my eyes.

## S<small>IMEON OF</small> S<small>ELEUCIA</small>

# I Ask Nothing More

I ask nothing more than to suffer
    for the cause of my Lord Jesus Christ
    and by this, to be saved.
If I can do this,
    then I can stand in confidence and quiet
    before the judgement seat of my God and Savior,
    when, in accordance with his will,
    this world passes away.

## Justin Martyr

*Saint Justin Martyr*
by Theophanes the Cretan (1545-46)

# With my Christ

With my Christ I have ever been,
With my Christ, I am now,
With my Christ, I will be forever;
In or out of suffering,
   you only will I confess.

## Nestor of Magydus

# A Stone Fit for Building

It has pleased you, Lord,
   to keep me until this time.
I thought, for a while,
   that you had rejected me as being
a stone not fit for your building;
   but now that you call me to take my place in it,
I am ready to suffer that I may have a part
   in your kingdom with all your saints.

## Serenus the Gardener

# An Exchange

Let the estates I own be ravaged,
   or given to others;
Let me lose my life, and
   let my body to be destroyed;
Rather than that I should speak one word
   against you, O Lord, who made me.
If they take from me a small portion
   of this earth and its wealth,
I shall exchange it for heaven.


Julitta of Caesarea

# True and Faithful Witness

Blessed be the God and Father
    of our Lord Jesus Christ,
who of his great and abundant goodness,
    willed that I should be a partaker
of the sufferings of his Christ
    and a true and faithful witness
of his divinity.

## Ignatius of Antioch

*Martyrdom of St Ignatius of Antioch*
by unknown artist (16th Century)

# I am a Christian

Lord, they ask me
   what I am.
I am a Christian.
I worship you, 0 Christ,
   the Son of God, for you came
   in these last days to save us,
   and you have delivered us from the
   snares of the wicked one.

## Carpus of Gurdos

# I Cannot Repay Such Mercy

The sins of my entire life,
   by which I have so often offended you,
my God, weigh me down like a mountain
   of my own making.
I wonder, 'What will be the end of all this'?
Yet, I do not lose hope.

I cannot bear this alone; I know I am weak.
But your strength will keep me from falling.
The prayers of others will
uphold me in my time of need.
I cannot repay such mercy;
to offer my life is only right.


John Ri

# You have Bound Me

I thank you, Lord and Master,
    that you have deemed to honor me
by making complete my love for you
    in that you have bound me with chains
of iron to your apostle Paul.

## Ignatius of Antioch

# He Heals by His Word

The physician our Savior
   is all powerful.
He restores those who worship
   the Lord and hope in him.
He heals not by men's cunning,
   but by his word.
Though he dwells in heaven,
   he is present everywhere.
All praise to him.

## Andronicus of Pompeiopolis

# Approach

The purpose of the Eucharist is to be a defense and a help for those who partake of it; therefore, we should strengthen those for whom we are concerned with armor of the Lord's Supper. How shall they be able to die for Christ, who are denied the blood of Christ? How shall they be prepared for drinking the cup of martyrdom, if we do not admit them beforehand to the chalice of the Lord?

## Cyprian of Carthage

*Chouans in the Vendee*
by unknown artist (19th Century)

# Introibo Ad Altare Dei...

I will enter unto the altar of God,
  to God who gives the joy of my youth.
Give judgement to me, 0 God,
  and defend my cause against the ungodly:
Deliver me from the wicked and deceitful person.
  For you are the God of my strength.
Send out your light and your truth,
  that they may lead me:
And bring me to your holy hill,
  to the place where you dwell.
I will enter unto the altar of God,
  to God who gives the joy of my youth.


NOEL PINOT (Psalm 43 adapted)

# You Know All About Me

O God, it was you who called me
    and sent me to this place.
You know all about me –
    the days I have lived
and the days that are left to me.
If it is your will to call me home,
    I leave the decision to you.

Yona Kanamuzeyi

# The Mere Shadow of Death

Lord, I am coming as fast as I can:
I know I must pass through the shadow of death
    before I can come to you;
But it is only the mere shadow of death,
    a little darkness upon nature:
But you, by your merits and passion,
    have broken through the jaws of death.

The Lord receive my soul, and have mercy upon me,
    and bless this kingdom with peace and plenty,
    and with brotherly love and charity,
that there may not be this effusion of Christian
    blood among them,
for Jesus Christ His sake, if it be your will.

Lord, receive my soul.

WILLIAM LAUD

# You Gave Strength

Lord God Almighty,
the Father of our Lord Jesus Christ,
You gave strength to your prophets
   and your holy apostles,
You gave strength to your holy martyrs,
May you also give strength to us,
   and protect us from harm.
Take our souls to yourself with our
   faces unashamed.
To you be glory, and to your beloved
   and holy Son Jesus Christ and the
   Holy Spirit, forever and ever.
Amen.

Paese the Copt

# Hear Us, O God

Hear us, O God, the Father of our Lord Jesus Christ.
Through your name the sea is calmed,
    the fire is quenched and the grave
    and death are brought to nothing;
You comfort those who are oppressed,
    you heal those who are suffering;
Those who are lost in the sea,
    you come to their aid;
In like manner, my Lord, also come
    to help us and deliver us from this time;
For you are the true God,
    the help of those who are oppressed
    and in tribulation,
    and yours is the power and the glory forever.
Amen.

## Shenoufe the Copt

# Direct our Steps

Lord, by your own hand you brought to light the eternal
   fabric of the universe and created the world of humankind.
From generation to generation you are faithful, right in your
   judgements, glorious in majesty and might.
You have created and established all that exists
   in wisdom and prudence.
To look about us is to see your goodness;
   To trust in you is to know your loving kindness.
0 merciful and pitying Lord, cleanse us from our sins
   and offenses, from our errors and failures.
Do not account every sin to your servants and handmaidens,
   but cleanse us by the power of your truth.
Direct our steps until we walk in purity of heart
   and our works are pleasing in your eye and in the sight
   of those who are our rulers.
Lord, show forth the light of your face upon us in peace
   for our help;
Shelter us by your mighty hand and save us from doing wrong
   by stretching forth your arm.
Deliver us from those who hate us without a cause;
To us and to all humankind grant peace and concord, even as you
   did to those who came before us when they called upon you
   truthfully and faithfully;
And cause us to be obedient both to your own almighty and
   glorious name, and to all who bear rule over us upon earth.

## Clement of Rome

# A Lost Sheep

Lord Jesus, I give you praise:
   I was a lost sheep, and you brought me back;
   I strayed from your flock, but your shepherd
   came and found me.
He sought me out, and brought me back to be offered
   with those sheep prepared for sacrifice.
I was returned to be a child of the apostles,
   a brother to those in the west who had
   received the crown, and an example to your
   people in the east.
Keep them all, do not let them lose the true faith.
Father, Son and Holy Spirit, true God, Glorious King,
   whom all that worship the Holy Trinity, in heaven
   and on earth, will ever confess, ages without end.
Amen.

## Gustazad of Seleucia

# Allow Me to Share

To those who are tried by the tempest, you are the calm harbor;
    you are the object of all that hope.
To those who are sick, you are health;
    you guide the blind and give help to those in need.
To those who face suffering, you always grant mercy,
    you are a light in darkness, a place of rest for the weary.

You brought forth the land, you rule the sea, all creation
    is set in its place by you;
By your word the heavens and the stars were created
    and made complete.
Noah was kept safe and Abraham given increase by you.
Isaac was released and a sacrifice was provided by you.
Jacob found sweet confusion as he struggled with you.
Lot was delivered from the judgement of Sodom by you.
You allowed Moses to see you, and you gave wisdom to Joshua.
Your mercy attended Joseph in exile, and you brought your people
    out from the land of Egypt.
You led your people into the land which you had promised them.
The three children in the furnace were protected by you,
    they were covered by your dew and the flames could not do
    them any harm.
Daniel was sustained and given life, for you closed the
    mouths of the lions.
Jonah was not allowed to die in the sea, for when the leviathan
    caught him, you allowed him to escape unharmed.
Judith was given the weapons she required; Susanna was delivered
    from the unjust judges by you.
You gave Escher her triumph; you cast down Aman.
You have delivered us from darkness into light eternal, your
    unquenchable light,
Father of our Lord and Savior Jesus Christ;
You gave to me the sign of the cross - the sign of Christ.

(cont. next page)

I ask you, Lord, do not count me unworthy of the suffering
    that has been endured by my brothers.
Allow me to share the crown with them.
Allow us to be together in glory as we have been
    together in prison.
Allow me to find my rest with them, as we have confessed your
    glorious name together.

# Severus of Thrace

# Grant Peace to Your Church

Lord Jesus Christ, creator of heaven and earth;
   you will never abandon those who put their trust in you.
We give you thanks:
   you have prepared us to live in your heavenly city
   and share in your kingdom.
We give you thanks:
   you have strengthened us to overcome the serpent
   and crush its head.
Grant rest to your servants,
   let the violence of their enemies be placed upon me.
Grant peace to your Church;
   may it be delivered from the oppression of the Wicked One.

## Theodotus of Ancyra

# Simple Faith

Lord Jesus Christ, when the desire is from the heart,
   you account it as the deed.
When the hindrance to its reality is only the inability
   to carry out the deed,
   we know that the intention alone is sufficient.
Although you have given us the power to choose what
   we might wish to do,
   the power to bring that choice to reality is yours alone.
May the simple faith of your servant Rogatian
   [although he is unbaptized] be accounted as though
   it were the gift of baptism;
And, if tomorrow the governor is insistent and puts
   us to the sword,
May the shedding of your servant's blood be for him
   as though it were the sacrament of anointing.

## Donatian of Nantes

# Nothing Greater

I enjoy life;
   but love of life has not
   made me afraid to die.
There is nothing greater than life ~
   that eternal life which gives
      immortality to the soul of the righteous.


Apollonius the Apologist (attributed)

# The Ladder

A ladder is before me, surrounded by light,
    stretching from the earth to heaven.
I am called by my friend to climb
    and not to fear.
I shall not die, but live and reign
    eternally with you, 0 God,
      and Jesus Christ your Son.

SADOTH OF SELEUCIA

# In Company with God

Near to the sword,
   I am near to God;
In the company of wild beasts,
   I am in company with God.
Only let all that happens be in the
   name of Jesus Christ,
     so that we may suffer with him.
I can endure all things if he enables me.

## Ignatius of Antioch

# Prayer for the Church

Good God, may we confess your name
   to the end;
May we emerge unmarked and glorious
   from the traps and darkness of this world.
As you have bound us together
   by charity and peace,
And as together we have persevered
   under persecution,
So may we also rejoice together
   in your heavenly kingdom.

## Cyprian of Carthage

*Saint Cyprian*
by Master of Messkirch (1535/ 40)

# A Branch of the Tree

This death, which seems so terrible,
   is little enough to gain eternal life.
Savior, receive a branch of the tree;
   it will decay, but will flower again
   and be clothed with glory.
The vine dies in winter, yet revives in spring.
Shall not this life which is cut down rise again?
My heart rejoices in the Lord,
   and my soul has exulted in your salvation.

James Intercisus

# He is Present

I pray God that the Church may be preserved
   immovable and steadfast in the true faith.
As to this wretched body, God will have care of it.
He is present and at hand; why should I be distressed?
I hope in his mercy that he will not prolong my course.

## Martin, Bishop of Rome

# You have Called Me

Lord, you have shown me
   what I must suffer.
As a dove descending,
   offering me food that is sweet,
So I know that you have called me
   and honored me with a martyr's death.

## Philip of Heraclea

# Beyond the Gates of Life

Blessed Father, eternal,
 binding all creation together
 by your strength,
Taking the heavens for your abode:
May we also pass beyond the gates of life,
 welcomed by you, 0 Father, and your Son.

## Methodius of Olympus

# The Conflict Closed

You are God of all,
  and to you belongs glory and praise,
because it has pleased you that we should
  carry on to its close the conflict that we
  have entered,
and that we should receive at your hands
  the brightness that shall never fade away.
God and Father of our Lord Jesus Christ,
  in peace receive our spirits to yourself.

## Shamuna of Sarcicitua

# The Eleventh Hour

Christ, forgive me for all of the sins I have
  committed against you,
  and all the times I provoked your anger by offering
  sacrifices to dead idols;
Have pity upon me and save me.
Deliver me from the judgement to come.
Be merciful to me, as you were merciful
  to the penitent thief
Receive me, like those who have turned to
  you, as you have turned to them.
I have entered your vineyard at the eleventh hour,
  deliver me from judgement.
Let your death, which was for the sake of sinners,
  restore me to life again in the day of your coming.

## Sharbil of Edessa

*The Stoning of St Stephen*
by Annibale Carracci - 1603-04

# Forgiveness

Lord Jesus, receive my spirit.
Lord, do not place this sin against them.

### Acts 7:59 - 60

# Lord, Bless...

Lord Jesus, you prayed for those who placed you
   upon the cross and told us to pray for our enemies.
Stephen, your deacon, prayed for those who put him to death,
   and. you received his spirit.
Receive the souls of my brother and receive my spirit
   with theirs.
Set us among the martyrs who have come before us and have
   received the crown of victory;
Set us among the holy apostles and blessed prophets.
Lord, bring to faith those who persecute us and put us
   to death, and do not count this against them as sin.
May they come to the knowledge that you are God.

Lord, bless all those in this land that you entrusted
   to my care.
Protect all the faithful as the apple of your eye.
In the midst of all these troubles,
   may they find shelter under the shadow of your wings.
Stay with them until the end of the age, as you promised.

Lord, bless this city that has witnessed our capture
   and our crowning.
I pray that your cross may keep it true to the faith
   now and forever.
Amen.

## Simeon of Seleucia

# Viva Cristo Rey!

May God have mercy on you!
May God Bless you!

Lord, you know that I am innocent.
I forgive my enemies with all my heart.
Hail, Christ, our King.


Michael Pro

# THEY ARE UNAWARE

I beg you, Lord God our Father,
Forgive them,
> for they are unaware of what
> they are doing.

## JAMES THE JUST

*James the Just, Lord's brother*
by Unknown Russian icon painter, 1809

# Release your Servants

Thanks be to God.
O Christ, Son of God, deliver your servants
    by the power of your name.
O God most high, do not consider the actions of
    my persecutors as sin.
God, have pity upon them.

Lord, for the sake of your name,
    grant me the strength to endure what I must.
Release your servants from the captivity of this world.
My God, I thank you,
    though I cannot thank you as I should.


Thelica of Abitine

# Remember

O Lord, remember not only the men and women of good will,
   but also those of ill will.
But, do not remember all of the suffering they have
   inflicted upon us:
Instead remember the fruits we have borne because
   of this suffering -
our fellowship, our loyalty to one another, our humility,
   our courage, our generosity,
the greatness of heart that has grown from this trouble.

When our persecutors come to be judged by you,
   let all of these fruits that we have borne
   be their forgiveness.


Anonymous - found in the clothing
   of a dead child at Ravensbruck
   concentration camp

# Not from my Enemies

Lord Jesus Christ,
   who came to this world as a man
and suffered your passion,
   allowing your hands to be nailed to the cross
   for our sins,
give me the strength to endure my passion.
It comes not from my enemies,
   but from my own brother:
Yet, Lord, do not account it to him as sin.

# Boris of Kiev

*Saints Boris and Gleb*
by unknown icon painter, (mid 14th century)

# IMITATION

There are different kinds of martyrdom,
namely, innocence, as in Abel;
uprightness, as in the prophets and John the Baptist;
love of the law, as in the Maccabees;
confession of faith, as in the apostles.

For all these various causes Christ the Lamb
is said to have been 'slain from the foundations
of the world'.

## THE DIALOGUE OF CAESARIUS

# Take Me to Yourself

I give you thanks, Lord Jesus Christ:
In the midst of my trials and suffering
   you have granted me the strength not to waver;
By your mercy, you have given me a share of glory eternal.

Lord Jesus Christ, your compassion caused you to suffer
   to save the world.
May the heavens open and the angels receive my spirit,
   for I am suffering for you and your church in this place.
I beseech you, merciful Lord, please take me to yourself
   and strengthen the faith of your servants who remain.

## Irenaeus of Sirmium

# Benediction

Blessed are you, Lord Jesus Christ,
  Son of God,
for you have, in your mercy,
  been so kind
as to allow me a death like yours.

## Papylus of Thyateira

*Thyatira by Arundell* in A dictionary of the Bible by Philip Schaff (1887)

# At Last

Now at last I am beginning
   to be a disciple.
No earthly pleasure can
   bring me any good,
     no kingdom of this world.
It is better for me to perish
   and obtain Jesus Christ
     than to rule over
       the ends of the earth.
Let me win through to the Light;
   that done, I shall be complete.
Let me suffer as my Lord suffered.

## Ignatius of Antioch

# An Offering by Fire

I thank you, Lord Jesus Christ,
   for your goodness in accepting me,
   an offering by fire for your name's sake:
   for you offered yourself upon the cross
   as a sacrifice for the sins
   of all the world.
I offer myself in death to you,
   who lives and reigns with
   the Father and the Holy Spirit,
   ages without end.
Amen.

# Afra of Augsburg

*Heilige Afra*
by Master of Messkirch (1535/40)

# Into your Hands

Into your hands, O Lord,
   I commend my spirit.
For the name of Jesus,
   and in defense of the Church,
   I am willing to die.

## Thomas á Becket

# Unworthy Though I May Be

I will always bless you,
    Lord Jesus Christ, Son of God:
For you have considered me as
    as being fit to share your fate,
Unworthy though I may be.


## Carpus of Gurdos

# Consummation

What then can separate us from the love of Christ?
Can affliction or difficulty?
Can persecution, hunger, nakedness, danger, or the sword?
'We are put to death all the day long for your sake',
as Scripture says; 'we are prepared like sheep
for the slaughter' -
Yet, despite all that happens to us, victory is
ours through him who loves us.
For I am fully assured that neither life nor death,
nor powers in the world, nor out of the world,
nor the heights nor the depths of the universe -
no, nothing in all that is created can separate
us from the love of God in Jesus Christ our Lord.

Romans 8:15 - 19

*Martyrdom of St. Paul*
by Joseph Martin Kronheim (1887)

# You have Thought Me Worthy

Lord God Almighty, Father of your beloved and blessed Child Jesus Christ, through whom we have come to have full knowledge of you - God of angels and power and of all creation, and of all the family of the just who live before you: I bless you that you have thought me worthy of this day and this hour, that I may be able to share in the number of the martyrs, to drink from the cup of your Christ, that I may rise and live forever, body and soul, in the incorruption of the Holy Spirit.

May I be admitted with those martyrs to your presence this day, as a welcomed and acceptable sacrifice. You have made my life a preparation for this; you let me see that this was to happen, and now you have brought it to pass, for you are the true and faithful God. For this and for all things, I praise you and give you glory, through the everliving high priest, Jesus Christ the heavenly, your dear Son. He is with you and the Holy Spirit. Through him may you receive glory now and forever. Amen.

## Polycarp of Smyrna

# On the Other Side

Blessed are you Lord,
    and may your Son's name
    be blessed forevermore.
I can see what those who
    persecute me cannot:
On the other side of this river
    there is a multitude
Waiting to receive my soul
    and carry it to glory.

## Sabas the Goth

# You have Heard Us

You have heard us,
    0 king of those in heaven and earth;
You have not allowed us to be
    put to shame;
But you have brought us and all
    who hear you to glory;
For you alone are God in heaven and earth
    with your beloved Son, Jesus Christ.

## Shenoufe the Copt

# The Crown

My Lord Jesus Christ,
Even as you have heard my brethren entreating you,
 and have accepted their sacrifice,
Even so, hear me when I cry to you;
May I also be counted worthy of the victor's crown
 which they have received.

## Sophia of Alexandria

*Les fortifications d'Alexandrie*
by Luigi Mayer (1803)

# Until my Enemies Know

God, hear me when I cry to you;
My Lord Jesus, do not forsake me,
   but come to me quickly;
For there is no God apart from you,
   be with me until my enemies know
   that you alone are God;
For yours is the power and the glory,
   forever and ever.
Amen.

## Pteleme the Copt

# Silence the Storm

Jesus Christ, Son and Word of God,
   hear me, your suppliant.
Silence the storm that rises against
   your church;
Let the pouring out of my blood,
   as your servant,
be a seal of the persecution of
   your flock.

## Peter of Alexandria

*View of Pompey's Pillar with Alexandria in the background*
by Cornelius de Bruyn (1681)

# Life Beyond Death

Lord Christ, I ask only that I might have
 the strength to endure what I must.
Lord Christ, I put my trust in you that
 you will grant me life beyond death.

## Saturninus the Younger of Abitine

# Accept My Praise

O Christ, I implore you,
   accept my praise.
Christ, deliver me:
   It is for you that I suffer.
Lord Christ, the time of trial is short,
   I will endure it with joy.

## Emeritus of Abitine

# Let Me Not Be Put to Shame

Lord Christ, let me not be put to shame.
Christ, I beseech you,
   let me not be put to shame.
Christ, come to my aid,
   have pity upon me,
   let me not be put to shame.
Christ, I beseech you, give me the strength
   to suffer what I must for you.

## Dativus the Senator

# You are Merciful

Lord, I give you thanks.

You are merciful to grant me this release.
God, I give you thanks.
I have lived in this world for fifty-six years.
I have kept myself pure, I have followed the gospel,
    I have preached the faith,
    and I have taught nothing but the truth.
Jesus Christ, Lord God of heaven and earth,
    I give myself to you in sacrifice,
    for you are the eternal one.
Glory and power are yours and will be forever.
Amen.

Felix of Tibiuca

# An Incorruptible Crown

I go from a corruptible
  to an incorruptible crown;
Where no disturbance can be,
  no disturbance at all.

## Charles Stuart

*Portrait of King Charles I in his Robes of State*
by a follower of Sir Anthony van Dyck (1636)

# Seed Sown

Our life is seed,
    sown in the earth to rise again
    in the world to come,
Where we will be renewed by Christ
    in immortal life.
I did not frame this body,
    nor will I destroy it;
God, you gave me life,
    you will also restore it.

Jonas of Beth-Iasa

# Receive Now my Soul

O Lord, my creator, from my birth
 you have always protected me;
You have taken from me the love of the world
 and given me patience to suffer.
Receive now my soul.

## Agatha of Catania

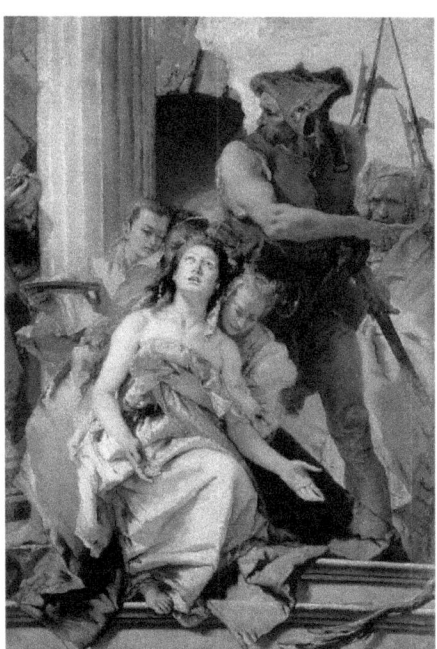

*The Martyrdom of St Agatha*
by Giovanni Battista Tiepolo (1750)

# I am God's Wheat

I am God's wheat.
May I be ground by
    the teeth of the wild beasts,
Until I become
    the fine white bread
That belongs to Christ.

## IGNATIUS OF ANTIOCH

# To Die for You Is to Live

Lord, teach me your wisdom.
Let all my members truly belong to you
   in this time of sacrifice.
You alone are the true God, for you alone
   I will suffer and die.
To die for you is to live.

## Arcadius of Caesarea

# Shelter

My God, shelter my children,
   for I am being taken from them.
Help me, Lord Jesus,
   since I bear this suffering for you.

Agathonice of Pergamos

# Prayer from Prison

The hour for my departure is upon me.
   I have run the race,
   I have finished my course,
   I have kept the faith.
Now, the prize awaits me,
   the crown of righteousness,
Which the Lord, the righteous judge,
   will award me on that day;
And not me only, but all who love his appearing.

. . . I was rescued out of the lion's jaws.
The Lord will rescue me
   from all evil,
   and take me safely into his
   heavenly kingdom.
To him be glory forever
   and ever! Amen.

## 2 Timothy 4:8, 18

# The Beginning

This is the end,
   but for me
It is the beginning
   of life.

**Dietrich Bonhoeffer**

# Last Prayer

I have been too long
   in this world of strife;
I would be with Jesus.

## Julian of Brioude

# Come to Help Me

Lord, Lord, Lord,
   please come to help me;
I turn to you alone
   for my refuge.

Agathonice of Pergamos

# Epilogue

How long, Sovereign Lord,
> holy and true
> must it be before you
> vindicate us . . .

## Revelation 6:10

*The Last Judgment*
by Michelangelo di Lodovico Buonarroti Simoni (1536-41)

# God's Church...
# Will Never Perish

Martyrdom is a grace of God that
   I do not believe I deserve.
But if God accepts the sacrifice of my life,
   let my blood be a seed of freedom
   and the sign that hope will soon be reality.
Let my death, if it is accepted by God,
   be for my people's freedom and a witness of hope.

You may say, if they succeed in killing me,
   that I pardon and bless those who do it.
Would, indeed, they might be convinced not
   to waste their time.
A bishop will die, but God's Church,
   which is the people, will never perish.


## Oscar Romero

# A Father's Prayer Upon the Murder of his Son

O God
We remember not only our son but also his murderers;
Not because they killed him in the prime of his youth and
　　made our hearts bleed and our tears flow,
Not because with this savage act they have brought further
　　disgrace on the name of our country among the civilized
　　nations of the world;
But because through their crime we now follow thy footsteps
　　more closely in the way of sacrifice.
The terrible fire of this calamity burns up all selfishness
　　and possessiveness in us;
Its flame reveals the depth of depravity and meanness and
　　suspicion, the dimension of hatred and the measure of
　　sinfulness in human nature;
It makes obvious as never before our need to trust in God's
　　love as shown in the cross of Jesus and his resurrection;
Love which makes us free from hate towards our persecutors;
Love which brings patience, forbearance, courage, loyalty,
　　humility, generosity, greatness of heart;
Love which more than ever deepens our trust in God's final
　　victory and his eternal designs for the Church and
　　for the world;
Love which teaches us how to prepare ourselves to face our
　　own day of death.

(cont. next page)

O God
Our son's blood has multiplied the fruit of the Spirit in
    the soil of our souls;
So when his murderers stand before thee on the day of judgement
Remember the fruit of the Spirit by which they have enriched
    our lives.
And forgive.

# Hassan Dehqani-tafti of Iran

# A Prayer of Thanks

We thank you, O God, for the saints of all ages;
For those who in times of darkness kept
   the lamp of faith burning;
For the great souls who saw visions of
   larger truth and dared to declare it;
For the multitude of quiet and gracious souls
   whose presence has purified and sanctified the world;
And for those known and loved by us,
   who have passed from this earthly fellowship
   into the fuller light of life with you.

Anonymous

# Those who Pray

Seeing that we are surrounded by so great a cloud of witnesses, let us set aside every weight and all that hinders us, and run with patience the race that is set before us.

## Hebrews 12: 1

*The Christian Martyrs' Last Prayer*
by Jean-Léon Gérôme (1863-83)

AFRA OF AUGSBURG was arrested as a Christian during the persecution of Diocletian and was put to death by burning in c. 304.

AGATHA OF CATANIA in Sicily is believed to have died under torture, having been arrested as a Christian during the early years of the fourth century.

AGATHONICE OF PERGAMOS was martyred in either the late second or mid-third century, along with her companions Papylus of Thyateira and Carpus of Gurdos in Pergamos. Accused of being Christians, they were examined, tortured, and killed. An exact account of the trial is preserved.

ANDRONICUS OF POMPEIOPOLIS in Cilicia was arrested as a Christian during the persecution of Diocletian, along with two companions in about 304. Following three examinations under torture, they were sentenced to be killed by wild beasts in the arena.

APOLLONIUS THE APOLOGIST is believed to have been martyred under Commodus, c. 185.

ARCADIUS OF CAESAREA in Mauritania was arrested as a Christian during either the persecution of Valerian or Diocletian. He was put to death by dismemberment.

THOMAS A BECKET, c. 1118-1170, became Archbishop of Canterbury in 1162. Following a long controversy with Henry II over the independence of the church from secular control, Becket was murdered in his cathedral by agents of the king on December 29, 1170.

DIETRICH BONHOEFFER, 1906-1945, was a German Lutheran pastor and theologian. Involved in the Confessing Church and anti-Nazi activities in wartime Germany, he was arrested in 1943. For two years he was held in a variety of prisons and concentration camps. On April 9, 1945 he was hanged in Flossenburg concentration camp by the personal order of Heinrich Himmler.

BORIS OF KIEV was the son of Vladimir, the first Christian prince of Kiev. He was put to death in 1015 by his eldest brother Svyatopolk who was an enemy of the new faith.

FRANCIS DE CAPILLAS was a French Jesuit sent as a missionary to Asia in the seventeenth century. He was tortured and beheaded during the Chinese dynastic wars of 1648.

CARPUS OF GURDOS (see above, AGATHONICE OF PERGAMOS)

CLEMENT OF ROME is believed to have been the third bishop of that city after the apostle Peter. He is thought to have been martyred at about the turn of the second century.

CRISPINA OF THAGARA in North Africa was arrested as a Christian during the persecution of Diocletian. Following a public trial she was condemned to death and beheaded in Theveste on December 5, 304.

CYPRIAN OF CARTHAGE in North Africa was the bishop of that place from c. 248 until his death. During the Decian persecution in the autumn of 249, he was forced to flee Carthage until 251. When the Valerian persecution reached the city in 258, Cyprian was arrested and put to death by beheading on September 14th of that year.

DATIVUS THE SENATOR (see below, THELICA OF ABITINE)

HASSAN DEHQANI-TAFTI, was the exiled bishop of the Episcopal Church in Iran. Before being forced to flee Iran with his family in the midst of the Iranian Islamic revolution, the bishop's son, Bahram, was dragged from his car and shot by members of the Revolutionary Guard on May 6, 1980.

DONATION OF NANTES was martyred along with his unbaptized brother, Rogation, c. 289.

EMERITUS OF ABITINE (see below, THELICA OF ABITINE)

EUPLUS THE DEACON was beheaded at Catania in Sicily under Diocletian, c. 304.

FELIX OF TIBIUCA was the bishop of that place in North Africa. He was martyred during the Diocletianic persecution, c. 304.

FERREOLUS OF VIENNE in Gaul is believed to have been martyred by beheading during a local persecution of the third century.

GENESIUS OF ROME had been an actor. One tradition indicates that he was converted to Christianity while acting in a pagan parody about martyrdom. He is believed to have been martyred under the emperor Diocletian, c. 285.

GUSTAZAD OF SELEUCIA (see below, SIMEON OF SELEUCIA)

HIPPOLYTUS OF ROME, c. 170 - c. 116, was an ecclesiastical writer and theologian of the early church. He is believed to have been martyred during the persecution of Maximin, along with several other leading clerics from the Roman church, c. 236.

IGNATIUS OF ANTIOCH, c. 35 - c. 107, was the bishop of that community in Syria. Arrested during a persecution of Christians in Syria he was taken to Rome for execution. On the journey he wrote a number of letters to churches in Asia Minor in which he reflected on the nature of the Church and his impending martyrdom. It is believed that he met his death in the Roman arena after having been exposed to wild beasts.

JAMES INTERCISUS was martyred during the second great persecution of Christians which took place in Persia, beginning in about 420. He was put to death by dismemberment.

IRENAEUS OF SIRMIUM was the bishop of that place (in present-day Hungary) and was martyred under Diocletian, c. 304.

JAMES THE JUST was a leader of the early Church in Jerusalem along with Peter, and appears to have acted as its president or bishop (cf. Gal. 1:19 - 2: 12). He was put to death by the Sanhedrin in 62, by being thrown from the city walls.

JANUARIUS OF CORDOVA in Spain was arrested as a Christian during the persecution of Diocletian, along with two companions. After having their faces disfigured, Januarius and his companions were martyred by fire, c. 304.

JONAS OF BETH-IASA, a monk in Persia, was arrested while offering comfort to Christian prisoners during the persecution of Sapor I in 327. After being tortured, he was executed along with a fellow monk by being crushed to death.

JULIAN OF BRIOUDE in Gaul is believed to have been a soldier converted to Christianity in the third century. During a local persecution he surrendered himself to the authorities and was beheaded.

JULITTA OF CAESAREA in Cappadocia was a wealthy widow arrested under the edicts of Diocletian as a Christian. She was condemned to death by fire in c. 303.

JUSTIN MARTYR, c. 100 - c. 165, was an early Christian apologist and author. He and his followers were arrested, perhaps at the instigation of the Cynic philosopher Crescens, scourged and beheaded, c. 165.

YONA KANAMUZEYI , c. 1918 - 1964, was a priest of the Anglican Church in Rwanda. During an incursion of terrorists,

Fr. Kanamuzeyi, as a prominent Christian pastor and supporter of the new republic, was kidnapped and shot.

WILLIAM LAUD, 1573 - 1645, Archbishop of Canterbury from 1633. Imprisoned in 1641, he was executed on 1 of January 1645. In his death he declared his adherence to the Church of England.

LUCIAN OF ANTIOCH, a priest in that city, was arrested under the edict of Diocletian and was imprisoned for nine years in Nicomedia. He suffered martyrdom on January 7, 312.

MARTIN, BISHOP OF ROME, was arrested in the midst of the Monothelite controversy by order of the emperor and banished to the Crimea where he died in captivity in 655. He is the last bishop of Rome to be remembered as a martyr.

METHODIUS OF OLYMPUS was bishop in Lycia. A theologian and poet, he is believed to have died in the Diocletianic persecution, c. 311.

GABRA MICHAEL was an Ethiopian convert to the Roman Catholic Church. Arrested, owing to his faith, by Theodore II, he died in his chains on August 28, 1855.

MONTANUS and his companions were arrested in North Africa during the persecution of Valerian. After an imprisonment of several months, they were executed by beheading in 259.

THOMAS MORE, 1478 – 1535, Lord Chancellor of England under Henry VIII, refused to accept the parliamentary Act of Supremacy on grounds of conscience. He was beheaded on Tower Hill on July 6, 1535.

NEMESIAN OF NUMIDIA was the bishop of that region and was arrested during the persecution of Valerian in 257. Along with a large number of his flock, he was banished to the mines and died there from ill-treatment.

NESTOR OF MAGYDUS was the bishop of that place in the region of Pamphylia and Phrygia. He was arrested during the reign of Decius and refused to renounce his faith. Nestor was executed by crucifixion in 251.

PAESE THE COPT is said to have been tortured and beheaded along with his sister Thecla during the Diocletianic persecution in Egypt during the early years of the fourth century.

PAPYLUS OF THYATEIRA (see above, AGATHONICE OF PERGAMOS)

PETER OF ALEXANDRIA was bishop of that city from 300 to 311. He was beheaded by the order of Maximin on November 25th, 311, having suffered a number of years both in prison and at forced labor.

PHILIP OF HERACLEA, the leading bishop in Thrace was arrested as a Christian during the persecution of Diocletian along with a number of his clergy. Following a period of imprisonment and physical abuse, the bishop and a number of his flock were put to death by burning in 304.

NOEL PINOT was arrested while celebrating the Eucharist in Paris at the time of the French Revolution. After twelve days in prison he was taken out, still in his vestments, to meet his death. As he mounted the guillotine on February 21, 1794 he was heard to recite the prayers usually offered by a priest at the foot of the altar.

POLYCARP OF SMYRNA, c. 69 - c. 1551 was bishop of that city and a leading Christian figure in Roman Asia. At the age of eighty-six he was arrested during a pagan festival. When he refused to renounce his faith, he was burned to death.

MICHAEL PRO (Michael Augustine Pro-Juarez) 1891- 1927, was a member of the Society of Jesus and an associate of the Young Christian Workers movement. Active in Mexico following the 1924 revolution, during which time religious orders were illegal, he was arrested owing to his church work. On November 23, 1927, he was executed by a firing squad.

PTELEME THE COPT was a martyr of the church in Egypt. According to one tradition, having been imprisoned and blinded, he was beheaded during the Diocletianic persecution in the early years of the fourth century.

QUIRINUS OF SISCIA was bishop of that city in Croatia during the time of Diocletian. After his arrest and examination, he was executed by drowning in c. 308.

JOHN RI, an associate of the Paris Foreign Missions, was martyred in Korea along with dozens of other Roman Catholic missionaries, clerics, and converts during the violent persecutions of 1839.

OSCAR ROMERO, 1917-1980, was the Roman Catholic Archbishop of El Salvador. A champion of the rights of the poor, an opponent of the military dictatorship, and an advocate of the pastoral mission of the Church, Romero was assassinated by a right-wing military group while celebrating the Eucharist on March 24, 1980.

SABAS THE GOTH died in the persecutions in Dacia (present-day Rumania) that took place under the Gothic ruler of that region in the late fourth century. Sabas is believed to have been martyred by drowning in c. 372.

SADOTH OF SELEUCIA succeeded Simeon (see below) as bishop. Having served his flock for less than a year, he was martyred along with a large number of his clergy, between 342 and 344.

SERENUS THE GARDENER is said to have initially hidden during the persecution of Maximin in Dalmatia (present-day Serbia). When finally arrested, he was beheaded in c. 302.

**SEVERUS OF THRACE** was a priest of the church in Heraclea. He died c. 304 in the Diocletianic persecution.

**SHARBIL OF EDESSA** is counted as an early Syriac martyr, c. 112.

**SHAMUNA OF SARCIGITUA** is believed to have suffered martyrdom in the region of Syria during the early portion of the second century.

**SIMEON OF SELEUCIA** (Simeon bar Sabba'e) was the bishop of that community in Persia. He and his companions, among them Gustazad, were martyred in the persecutions instigated by Sapor II, between 339 and 341.

**CHARLES STUART**, 1600-1649, King of England, Scotland, and Ireland from 1625. He was executed on January 30, 1649 and is rightly considered a martyr, as his death was conditioned by his resolve to defend the Church.

**SATURNINUS THE YOUNGER OF ABITINE** (see below, THELICA OF ABITINE)

**SHENOUFE THE COPT**, according to the Coptic tradition preserved in the Pierpont Morgan codices, was arrested during the Diocletianic persecution along with eleven other members of his family. The entire family is said to have died under torture.

**SOPHIA OF ALEXANDRIA** is said to have been the sister of Shenoufe the Copt (see above).

**THELICA OF ABITINE** in North Africa was martyred with a number of companions in the Diocletianic persecutions, c. 304.

**THEODOTA OF PHILIPPOPOLIS** in Thrace is believed to have suffered in the insurrection of Licinius against Constantine the Great, c. 318. Following torture, she is supposed to have been stoned to death.

THEODOTUS OF ANCYRA is said to have been martyred along with seven companions in Asia Minor during the Diocletianic persecution, c. 303.

THEOPHANES VENARD was a missionary priest who served in French Indo-China (present-day Vietnam) in the nineteenth century. During a violent outbreak of persecution in Western Tonkin, he was arrested and following two months of captivity in an open cage, Venard was beheaded on February 2, 1861.

# You've Read the Story
# Now Listen to the Songs

Duane Arnold and Michael Glen Bell have collaborated to create a musical version of *Martyrs' Prayers*. To hear this unique music and to purchase an album, visit their website at

## www.themartyrsproject.com

Read on to learn the story behind The Project:

## THE MARTYRS PROJECT
## AND
## MARTYRS' PRAYERS

Long ago, but near in memory, we thought that we could change the shape of the Church and the world through music and the study of early Christian worship. We were young. We were confident. We were brash. We were friends.

In a small Ohio fellowship of believers, we would play host (often for days or weeks at a time) to Larry Norman, Randy Stonehill, Daniel Amos, Phil Keaggy, The Talbot Brothers, Jessy Dixon, Rez Band, and Petra (to name a few), all the while reading ancient Christian writers, listening to Robert Webber and trying to discover the meaning of worship and communion. Set next to racks of Rolling Stone magazine and the latest albums ranging from The Eagles to Iggy Pop, it was a heady mix. In the end, it could not last. So, we all went our separate ways. The dream had died, but, at least by two of us, it was not forgotten.

We lost touch with each other, and with the contemporary Christian music scene, as we set off to graduate schools, postings overseas and lives within mainline denominations. We could not, however, forget our friendship or the forces that had shaped us.

In 2010, I reconnected with my old friend, Michael Glen Bell. We were together again. After draining the dregs of nostalgia and rejecting all the current descriptions of our theological positions - emergent, post-evangelical, neo-orthodox, etc. - we wondered if there was a way by which we could express our love of the Church and our love of music with content? Could we send a "love note" in a musical form to all of those who are just like us all over the world - displaced Evangelicals, or Evangelical Catholics, who remember what was, who see what is, and who want something more?

We decided to record an album based on the prayers of the martyrs, the prayers you have read in this book.

In turning our attention to the prayers of the martyrs we agreed with our old friend, Kemper Crabb, who has expressed his approach in this way:

> A brute retrieval of the ancient is not enough. As Geoffrey of Vinsauf wrote in Poetria Nova, his 13th Century book on the art of rhetoric:
>
> "Permit an old word to regain its youth by giving it a home in another situation where it can be a novel guest, giving pleasure by its strangeness."
>
> Those vital things which have been allowed to sink into obscurity must be resurrected, though in a fashion which renders them accessible and attractive to an age which has forgotten them.

"To an age which has forgotten..." Currently Christian music is an industry. It is not a cause, not a catalyst for change and certainly not a challenge to the Church at large. It is no longer counter-cultural. It rarely asks questions. It seldom inspires. It no longer gives "pleasure by its strangeness". Whether we have done something different in our musical endeavor will be decided by you - the reader and the listener.

As friendship lay at the heart of the project, we turned to friends to help us. Those friends, old and new, have shaped the music and us. The guitars of Phil Keaggy and Glenn Kaiser, the voices of Randy Stonehill and Margaret Becker, the sensibilities of Owen Thomas and Thom Daugherty (The Elms), the Muscle Shoals vocals of Wayne Berry, the passion of Jennifer Knapp, the gospel intensity of the McCrary Sisters, the gentle humanity of Kemper Crabb, the work of Mike Pachelli and the backbeat of John Sferra made this project a joy.

So, we offer this small effort of prayers and music to all of you, in the hope that the prayers of the martyrs may become a "novel guest", may ask a question and maybe even, might lead you home...

Duane W.H. Arnold

www.themartyrsproject.com

www.ingramcontent.com/pod-product-compliance
Lightning Source LLC
Chambersburg PA
CBHW070605050426
42450CB00011B/2997